Heartwork Therapy

Kayil York

OTHER BOOKS BY KAYIL YORK

Roses &Thorns
Bleeding Caverns
11:11
You Deserve More
Brave Soul

Kayil York

"Yes, you will rise from the ashes,
but the burning comes first.

For this part,
darling,
you must be brave."

—KALEN DION

Kayil York

*I dedicate this book to my own heart.
For the sacrifices it has made for the wellbeing of
my soul. I dedicate this book to the little girl and
now the grown woman, who always put others
before herself, who would give all of herself at the
expense of her own happiness, just to see others
smile. The one who opened her heart and her arms
for everyone even when she needed a heart and
arms to fall into herself. This book is for her and
all the words she left unspoken, until now. The
words spilled out effortlessly on these pages
because they came straight from the depths of her
soul. The words that needed to be spoken to realize
she never needed a round of applause from anyone
other than herself. This book is her own round of
applause, this book is her victory.*

Kayil York

Heartwork Therapy Playlist

"Depression" – Dax
"Face Down – Symphonic Edition" – The Red Jumpsuit Apparatus
"Sleepwalking" – All Time Low
"Tear Me to Pieces" – Story Of The Year
"Filthy Notes" – Lacrimas Profundere
"Dreamstate" – Dayseeker
"Machine" – Born of Osiris
"Sister of Charity" – The 69 Eyes
"hope ur happy" – Until I Wake
"Black Hole" – Our Mirage
"Without Me" – Dayseeker
"Thanks For Asking" – Five Finger Death Punch
"don't sleep, repeat (ft. MGK) – 44Phantom, Machine Gun Kelly
"Lost Myself To You" – Besomorph, Mougleta
"No More Tears To Cry" – Bullet For My Valentine
"Let It Go (with Lø Spirit)
"Fake" – Until I Wake
"Miracle" – A Day To Remember
"Razor's Edge (ft X Ambassadors) – Masked Wolf, X Ambassadors
"Strong for Someone Else" – The Lone Wolf
"Mindfields" – Faouzia, John Legend
"Separate Ways" – Eva Under Fire

Kayil York

DISCLAIMER

Be advised. This is a book of fiction, any relation that you find is merely coincidental. This book has adult language, mentally graphic adult situations, and uncomfortable topics.

Heartwork Therapy
By Kayil York
Copyright © 2023

Cover Art: Mitch Green
Radpublishing.co

Kayil York

*The mind cannot heal
without the healing of the soul.
And that kind of healing is one
you have to fight fear for.*

Before we begin this, understand that you are not your past. You are not the things that have happened to you. You are not the people who have wronged you. You are pre-destined for greatness that life prepares you for. The lessons you learn are for your future. Step by step you will walk through different kinds of fire that will threaten to destroy you. At times it will be so you can rise above the remnants of your old self to be brand new. You will change, your heart will remember the lessons and your soul will learn how to be someone even better. Your past will be left behind as you step forward with the new wisdom it taught you. You are no longer who you were yesterday; you are who you are *right now*. In this moment, in this time. You are exactly who you are meant to be and exactly where you are meant to be.

Some people will always choose to be the victim in every part of their story because they love being the monster. In the end, no one can save them from their own self destruction until they choose to face themselves and accept that they are the problem.

There will be people who will take your Genuity as toxicity—
You may mean well and do the best you can to do what's right, and they will still find a way to say you did it all wrong.

Kayil York

Forgiveness isn't band aids on bullet wounds.
It is balm thickly applied onto the wound.
The constant application of mending,
until there isn't any pain left when
you touch it.

Even though we may not understand sometimes, we must accept the hard things so we can process how to protect our hearts from the things that aren't for us.

Kayil York

Silence is deeply wounding.
It screams the answers, speaks the truth,
and tells me what I needed to hear
that words refused to voice.

Sometimes you are meant to stand alone.
Not because you're weak.
Not because you can't be around other people.
But because your purpose is a higher calling that requires a great deal more attention than what others can understand.

Don't underestimate the power of losing people who are not meant to have a place in your life. The knowledge you gain can be so much greater when they're gone compared to the lens you saw them through when they were present. Because we see them as they are, for who they are, rather than what we hoped them to be. And that is a powerful truth.

Healing is only impossible
to the people who avoids
the possibility of healing.

Each day comes with its own battles. The battle of trying to fight the pain, the hurt, the uncertainty of healing or finding peace. Some of those days come with a vengeance, and it is very difficult to get a grip on yourself. Because the anger can boil in your blood and spill into the minutes you thought you had it all together. It's ok to have this time of anguish and sorrow. Not every day is going to be a good day. Know that it is alright to be in this kind of space. Our life will have uncomfortable memories that we can't avoid. But the important thing to remember amidst the chaos, is the wisdom, understanding, and peace it brings when you make it through those challenging times.

It doesn't just go away, but it doesn't have to stay
and hurt.
That's the difference between pain and healing—
you can be in the presence of the cause yet choose
not to react out of pain.

The scars and craters formed on my heart are from every broken promise ever made to me. I only see the beauty. Because I am the master of my own phases. And I, like the moon, hold a beauty of my own.

I'm not sure how it's possible to become more sensitive and stronger at the same time. But somehow this kind of enhancement has made me better. I strive to be the best version of myself—and the more life that happens to you, the more growth you gain. I keep strength close to my heart, because for so long I spent too much time being soft. And when you're too soft, it becomes easy for the hardness to stay and invade.

Kayil York

I want to thank every person that has hurt me. Because you showed me how I could become better, where I can improve my wisdom, and what real connection is. Thank you for hurting me so I could see the truth that I was blinded to. I would not be where I am or who I am without your heart break.

I watched it all unfold before my eyes. It wasn't graceful, it wasn't beautiful, and it sure as hell didn't feel good. But keeping peace with myself was more important than holding onto someone who didn't care about treating me right. Ungracefully, unbeautifully, and in pain, I let you go. Not because I wanted to. But because I needed to.

Please do not insult me by telling me one thing while showing me something else completely. I have tried to read you the way you want, but it's impossible to see such fantasies. But I guess it makes sense, coming from someone who lives their life like it *is* a fantasy. Your whole life is made up of things that aren't real. So, I understand why you want me to believe the show you put on, but I wasn't made to live my life on wishful thinking and beautiful lies. I see through it all, I don't like it, and I don't need to have a relationship with someone who isn't real with me.

When the heart gave in and the soul opened, you reached right in and let your hurt lay out to them. There was a pact, you see, a kind of sick reverie. Given in shots of deadly sins that you only crave to drink in. But the war begins the moment you stop to see the damage that's been done. And when you decide to stop the madness, the flames erupt. The house burns down, and the pieces of yourself that you gave to it all has now turned to dust. They'll sit back in their fury and keep drinking the poison, because it's all they ever want to know. And how dare you leave such a space when everything was perfectly wrong?

-trauma bonds

You love me
you leave me-
you hate me
you want me-
you need me
then grieve me-
you pull me in
before you spit
me back out.

Now I'm dirty and exhausted.
My battle scars are nothing
but tales of love and loss.

No.
I will not water myself down to
make you feel better about yourself.
No.
I will not allow your words to make me feel like
I'm less than who I am.
No.
You will not have the kind of power over me that
tells me I am not good enough.
Because I am stronger than that.
Which makes me stronger than you.

One day you'll look back at this pain and it won't make you twinge the way that it used to. One day you'll look back at this wreckage and be grateful for the wound it forced you to learn from. Your vision will be so clear, and the things that were once a jumbled mess inside your head, will have unwound itself to show you why this ending was necessary. Because sometimes, my dear, the war is working to correct your vision because it wasn't where it needed to be in the first place. Even in the midst of this chaos, everything is working itself out to be the way that it needs to be. Keep pushing through so you can get to the part where it all becomes clear. It is worth it.

It doesn't need to hurt this much all the time. There is a reason you have a heart that puts itself back together again after it's been broken. You were born with a spirit of resilience. Even though the world tries to tear that from you to keep you in pieces, Keep fighting for the wholeness through your resiliency. Because as the healing comes, the pain subsides.

Kayil York

Nothing hurts more
than loving someone
while having to
let them go—

I wasn't going to let you ruin me.
I forgave myself instead of waiting for your forgiveness. I moved on so that brokenness wouldn't haunt me anymore.

Kayil York

There are never any uncertainties.
It's certainties that you're uncertain about.

Therapy is the mess we create
to bring the clarity we need.

I've made my peace not making amends with certain people. You can forgive without having reconciliation. Because the importance is your quality of life. Making peace with the ones who caused the destruction in the first place, is not an obligation you're entitled to. If it does not bring you peace, you don't have to subject yourself to it.

Habitual toxic behavior doesn't change.
They just find another way to present it to make you think this time would be different than the rest.
Don't be fooled. Patterns don't change.

Take a breath and close your eyes.
Whisper a prayer and remind yourself that it's going to be ok. Even if every bone, muscle, and emotion doesn't believe. Help yourself in believing it will become ok. Because this day has not defeated you. You still have the strength to power through the struggle of weariness.
Just believe in yourself.

In a world full of skin, I have pulled my own back so that when you see me, you see the bones of my soul and structure of what a heart is made of. Because when the years are over, there will be nothing left to gaze upon except for the truth of who you are without the shadow of your skin.

It's not weakness when you choose to start over. It's mature recognition that the way you were living was not serving you, challenging you, or making you better. And the moment you decide to step into that transition is the moment your fears become the collateral damage in this fight to being everything you were meant to be. That victory is worth the sacrifice.

It's ok to leave people behind. Not everyone is willing to step forward themselves when the going gets rough. But that doesn't mean you have to stay behind with them. And you shouldn't apologize for choosing to heal the parts of you that broke along the way.

Don't let them tell you
you're *worth it*
without *showing you*.

You keep me hoping that life has better things to offer than the pain that keeps crossing my path.
I am so grateful for that.

Stop making yourself small to fit into other people's worlds. I have learned over the years how diminishing it can be to try and piece yourself where you don't belong. it takes time to get to this place, where you aren't so worried about fitting in. Where you don't shift yourself to please other people. It takes strength to stand out in your own skin. Don't waste your life trying to be in places you don't belong, your purpose is greater than that. Stop making yourself small. Rise into your greatness and stand out in it.

What are we, but humans constantly pulling ourselves open to prove we can be more than the skin we're confined in.

You started to paint me black. Flicking your wrists with anger in each stroke, covering things up to see what you wanted to see instead of what was real. It wasn't until you stood back to recognize you were only covering up the distorted image of yourself.

—*projection*

I am not there anymore
I am not in that terrible chaos anymore
I am safe where I am
I am not going to come undone
I will not let this hurt, because it doesn't
I will not let this torment, it's not worth it
I am stronger than this feeling
And I will be ok

-in the midst of anxiety

Kayil York

I don't live in a world
where it's my job to make
sure I don't offend you.

Even though you have
so much to give,
remember
that not everyone
is deserving of it.

Kayil York

I needed you to give up on me,
because I would not have been able
to let you go if you didn't.

SHOW UP.
There comes a point where you need to show up for the ones who always showed up for you. The ones you promised your loyalty to, you need to prove from time to time.

I'm not going to keep destroying myself to please you. I'm going to stop trying to make you see that I am worthy of you when you keep pushing me away—

Your silence was screaming *NO*.
Your silence told me everything I needed.
I will not beg you to answer—
so don't be surprised when you no longer hear
from me. I must protect my heart from now on.

Walking away is not the same as stabbing someone in the back. Protecting yourself from harm is what it means to be safe. Anyone who says any different is trying to sell you something.

The narcissists play the victim.
They act like the pain they caused you,
is the pain you caused them.
They will love you to eventually hate you.
They are masters of their own destruction,
and a genius at making you believe that *you*
are the cause of their self-destruction.
They are the unstable ones who look
to torment the stable.
They are the thorn in your side that you don't
realize is the reason you're constantly bleeding.
They play the wicked game of hearts,
throwing them up *just to watch them shatter*.

I believed you again.

This time I thought it would be different than the thousand other times that you let me down.

I believed you.

This time I really thought we would change the way things had been. The way I had always imagined it.

I believed you. *I fucking believed you.*

And here I am again, getting my heart broken, again, because again, you don't show up.

Sometimes people really don't change.

The hard part about forgiving
is the decision to move passed
the pain that was holding you
back from forgiving in the first place.

Kayil York

Sometimes the magic you think is there
is really all in your head.
Because they stop texting you,
they stop calling,
they stop showing you
what you adamantly believed
was authentic connection.
And then they are gone,
as if it never happened
in the first place.

These pretty lies are so pretty.
But they won't be enough to
sway me to fall for them.

Sometimes I think it was all an undercover scheme. Because there was more investigating than there was the means in showing love. As if it was a game to see how much time had to go by before I fully gave myself over to you. Granted it didn't take much, and I was a fool for falling while you were focused on leaving. But I learned how to look out for people like you, so I won't be fooled again.

You broke my heart so intensely,
I had to learn how to breathe
right again—

Kayil York

It's so difficult
to accept an absence
you feel like you
could have prevented.

The strength of the heart
is one that time proudly holds
itself accountable for.

I write vows daily to myself. Because I have to commit to taking care of myself. I have to commit to making sure my mind is where it needs to be. I have to make sure my soul is full of the right kind of fuel. *Daily*. Because as I look around, too many of us are not committing to ourselves. We will up our hearts with temporary fixes and wonder why our souls are always empty, hungry, and broken.

Some people just have a gift of making all the
good things seem negative. And never stop to
think that maybe the reasons they see things
that way is because they never bothered to
try and see any of the good.

You failed to see how I always put your feeling before my own. Time and time again. But I had to stop when I realized you never did the same for me. And somehow it was my fault that I had to step back from you. It was my fault for seeing the boundaries you placed. It was my fault for protecting myself from someone who claimed to love me yet did nothing to show me.

-it was just always about you

I think about it more than I should. And I wish it would have been different. But it isn't.
It hurts most days.
And sometimes it really isn't ok that I lost you.
But the selfishness outweighed the selflessness.
And the lies were too much to try and pick through to understand. So, I did what I had to do, because it was my turn to put myself first.

The moment the consistency becomes inconsistent is the moment hope is crushed. I know it's difficult to keep your drive going for the things and the ones you love. But it is one of the best ways to show where you stand. If things need to change, at least have the common courtesy to say so or explain why. The worst thing you can do is become a ghost without warning or reason to someone who loves you. It seems to be the modern-day walking dead.

Because silence is an easier way to let things die, rather than trying to explain the truth of what you feel.

Looking back isn't the same as running back.

The difference is that you can look at all the things that have brought you to where you are now. Acknowledging the hurt that taught you important lessons. Reminding yourself how far you've come from where you were.

That is the right way to go about looking at your past. But trying to relive, revive, and reinvent your past, is an unhealthy act that may lead to self-destruction.

Let go of what has already happened, recognize the lessons in the mistakes, and apply the necessary tools that you've learned to the things of today. This is the way to go about living the way you should.

I am not a temporary love that you can leave and come back when it's convenient for you.
I am not the girl who's going to stress about not hearing from you.
I am not the girl who is going to try and convince you that I am worth your time.
I am not going to randomly show up when you're looking for an ego boost.
I am not going to sit around and wait for you to possibly show up when you say you might.
I am better than that.
I am deserving of time.
And to be seen as an equal, not mere collateral.
I deserve to be seen, I earned being heard.
And just in case you forgot, here's a reminder of who the fuck I am.

It's ok to ask for more,
it's ok to need more,
and it's ok to want it.
We are human,
and it's important
to voice the things
that we are lacking.
Because we are made
to soak up love like
a sponge, because it
is the reason we live.
the reason we breathe,
and how we have been
built up.

You wanted me to apologize for being the way that I am. But I can't do such a thing. I have worked so hard in my becoming. I have fought long and tirelessly to be all that I am. I make no apologies to you or anyone else for being exactly who I fought to be.

When will I stop feeling the need to hide?
How can I stop hiding what I feel?

When you start acting like someone who wants to be in light.

Kayil York

She learned that life isn't
about sharing your wings,
but about showing others
how to grow their own.

Some people create bonds by sharing their pain and traumas, while convincing themselves it's a true connection. And it may be that way for that time. But once you choose to enter the healing phase, the bond will come apart if you're the only one choosing to heal.

I never tried to be perfect, but you still screamed at my flaws, and rejected the way I tried to be humble when I did something wrong. You always said that no one could tell you what to do, yet you had no problem doing it to others.

All I wanted was for you to show a fraction of humility. Because when it came down to it, you chose your ego over it all. Laced it up your spine with fire and burned out everything that could possibly make you bend. The sad part of it was how easy it was for you to pretend the pieces of what was left of us didn't deserve a voice. I came to terms with your war, and the way the demons fought to keep me away. There was no coming back from this, I knew it in my bones. I set fire to our bridge
and walked the other way.

—defeated

Kayil York

I have spent my sleepless nights curled up
in the arms of ocean waves, desperately trying
to count stars to heavy my lids.
More times than not I find myself running my
hands over the canvas of the sky just to feel
the landscape beneath my fingers until
the end of the night.

Accepting what is no more is the hard part.
Because the notion of it all falling to pieces was never a part of the plan.

You didn't have to be so cold,
but it told me the truth of you.
The things you refused to say,
that time confessed to me.
I then understood what you
meant when you explained
that you would rather have
no one. I don't know why I
thought I could be an exception.

-I just hoped

Be proud of the way you broke.
It showed you a new place to grow from.

You don't just get there. Healing is a process. Living is a process. Achieving your goals is a process. It's something you will constantly be chasing, reaching for, and working on and through. You never get there, you just keep growing through, moving through, and getting to a higher level of accomplishment.

A simple reprieve from the pains of life is in the moments we stop to appreciate all the blessings we have.

It was *I* who needed saving from *you*.
Not the other way around.
You lost me because you stopped being honest about the things you needed.
You lost me because the desire to be closer to my family was greater than trying to be my friend.
You lost me because you didn't try to listen to me. You lost me because you made everything about you. You lost me because I wanted understanding and you spat back resentment.
You lost me because your hold of bitterness was coated in your words, and I could taste it.
You lost me because your negativity no longer resonated with me. And I had to cut out the roots that were holding me back, and it kills me it had to be you.

It probably never would have hit me if you didn't say anything, but I'm tired of being merely a choice of convenience when you're lonely. I let it be ok for far too long because of how much hope I had in us. In the love I thought was there, at least the love I had for you. I gave you too much of myself when you gave me pretty words disguised as hope. And the more closely I looked, the more I realized how little you were giving. I fooled myself into thinking it was something real, something deep, and now that someone else has come along stealing your heart away, I am back to the silence. But when it doesn't work out, and your loneliness creeps in, you can't come back to me with more pretty words trying to persuade me that you need me. Because I will have moved onto to someone who really cares about me around the clock and doesn't make me question his loyalty in the silence.

Don't get discouraged when you don't feel like you're moving in any direction. This is the time to contemplate, this is the time to pause, to take a breath from the madness.

Sometimes the pause is the next step.

It's difficult to deal with back-and-forth people.

At the start everything goes smoothly, you get along, you click, and the days seem to go by with more happiness than you thought was possible. For a while, things are well. Until someone's feelings get hurt. The offer of forgiveness isn't taken. Then you can't tell whether things are ok or not. Because they say one thing, but their actions are speaking another language. Then bitterness starts to dance, and resentment claps its hands, and it's hard to see where the missteps were. Where it all went wrong. No matter how much you try to talk about it, or try to come to a resolve, nothing can be done. Then it gets to the point of having to let go, because grace was not given. Understanding wasn't practiced. And the choice to try to reconcile was just a mirage in an already dry desert.

Give her some space to breathe. And before you make this about you, stop and think for a second. She's hurting in places that haven't been touched by pains hand and it's suffocating her. There is no capacity to take in anyone or anything that isn't helping her stop the destruction going on in her soul. This isn't the time to take away from her, she's already depleted. Fighting to keep any kind of piece from escaping the story that has built up her life. But it isn't the same. The cracks grew too wide on her landscape, painfully distorting everything she's ever known. If there was something you could do it would be to leave her alone here. This is a place you are not welcome at. She is searching for things you are not allowed to be a part of anymore. And the hard part isn't over yet. So let her be. You won't win this war because she took herself out of the line of fire. And she won't be coming back because she knows it's not worth returning to a place that does nothing but destroy your soul.

I just wanted you to show up for me. This was the time I needed you to show me that you are there for me. Over the years I was always there. Giving all that I could to show you how much I value you. I asked you to show up for me this once. I couldn't have stressed enough how much it meant to me to have you there. But you didn't answer. You didn't show up. It left a huge hole in my heart, a deep wound in my soul that I'm trying to maneuver through. I am entirely swollen with pain and I don't know how I'm going to come back from this.

Kayil York

I will let this pain go-
But I can't undo the changes
it's made to my heart.

It will be unbearable to endure something you thought you could never live without. It will hurt you more than you wish and take a long time to heal from. But in the same token, it will heal so well. The balm to your wounds will soothe the aches in time. It may not cure the loneliness, but it will make sure you know how strong you can be. Grab ahold of that strength and let that be the anchor that keeps the peace within you.

You will grow different towards your pain.

Some people will hate you for the only simple reason that despite their efforts to try and bring you down, you still choose to grow, thrive, and rise above them.

You were not wrong for choosing yourself.
But my dear, I was not wrong for choosing myself either. The difference is you took it as rejection instead of my need for self-progression.

When you are moving into healing, you must surround yourself with people who care and support that progression. Not everyone will be rooting for your success. Protecting your heart means being picky about who you let be close to you.

You must stop thinking about it so much.
The anxiety, the worry, the unknown.
It can become too attached to your home.
The last thing you need is for unwelcomed
things to be living in places they shouldn't.
Remind yourself that no matter what happens,
you will be ok. Things will work out the way
that they should. Even if it wasn't the way you
wanted it to work.
Remind yourself to stay calm. *Breathe*.
Then steer your thoughts to things that truly
matter, that give you peace, and understanding and
a means to move forward.

Remember that some people will accuse you of things that you haven't done. When that happens, it's usually because they are projecting their own insecurities and problems onto you.

I stopped being angry at you because I realized it
was your heart that wasn't right.

I could never fix that for you—
That's something I could never change
no matter how badly I wanted to.

Kayil York

Too many people are still hurting
because they are too afraid to face
the pain. What they don't realize
are the walls that get built,
the bitterness that takes root,
and the fear that grows like wildfire.
The more is spreads, the more it destroys.

Sometimes I am whole and healthy.
Sometimes I am nothing but bits and pieces.
Sometimes I am happy and glowing.
Sometimes I am broken and bleeding.
Sometimes the light is my strength.
Sometimes the dark is my therapy.

I am human when it comes down to it,
A complete juxtaposition of sorts.
A piece of Universe with bones
soaked in earth.

Kayil York

I don't know why I hold so much space for your memory. You have been gone for a long time, you no longer hold the weight that you used to, and I have no reason to remember you the way you used to be. Because you are no longer that same person. But the memory always remains.

Speak well over yourself.
Even though we are flawed,
we should still recognize
the beauty of who we are.
It will increase the love
we should be constantly
developing within ourselves.

Don't be ashamed of needing help.
Sometimes we can be so overwhelmed
with life that we need to have someone
to lean on.

Work on your heart and the things that it carries. Some things should not be there that you are holding space for that should be open for other things. Check in with your wounds to see what can be healed or restored. Then check in with your mind to see how removing those toxic things from your heart has shifted the way you think. It's important to see what changes, to recognize the progress of taking away what only harms. Be consistent in checking in with yourself. It's the best form of self-care.

Kayil York

There isn't time for me to wonder if what
you're saying is true. Time tells all.
I'll listen to what you say and watch
to see if it comes to life or not.

Healing has a way of fixing the way you used to see things. In hindsight, you're able to recognize the issues that got you hurt in the first place. Now that you see those areas, you know where to work on yourself so that you don't find yourself with the same hurt the next time that situation tries to reappear.

I am never your priority. I am the option you need when there hasn't been enough love to go around from the people that aren't me. Maybe it's my fault because I told you I would always be here, but I guess I should put my foot down because you come back to break my heart and don't even know it while you walk out the door. You turn your face so fast to avoid seeing the tears making bruises on my chest. I shouldn't be surprised this cycle hasn't been broken, but I feel too weak to tell you no. Because my heart is always louder with the *maybe* over the warnings in my head. But the next time will be different, I promise. Because I'm learning to say no to what sucks the life from me. What drains me. And what hurts me.

I recognized it for what it was
and said my last goodbye.
There is no use dealing with hearts
that only wish to burn you down.

Kayil York

In life, the hardest thing you can do
is accept yourself for who you are,
being all that you are.

Do not pursue someone's heart
when you have no intention
of loving them right.

Kayil York

I don't need saving.
I just want someone to
be by my side to help me
get through when it doesn't
feel like I can do it alone.

It amazes me how much you learn
with every failure that happens.
Yes, it doesn't feel good to fall.
But at least you know how to do
better the next time life tries
to knock you down.

It's ok to walk away because they kept failing to listen. It's ok to walk away when the excuses are far greater than the effort. It's ok to walk away when the behavior has stayed the same, and the idea of change is just manipulation. It's ok to walk away when they stop trying on purpose, while purposely denying it. It's ok to walk away when you've done everything you can to make things work and the result leaves you back where you started.

Give chances.
But don't allow them to take
advantage of your grace.
Those who are truly sorry
will change their behavior.
Those who are using you,
will repeat the offenses.

Narcissists. You can't talk to them about your feelings because they find a way to turn the tables on you. This is not someone who is truly for you. Real people will listen and try to understand where you are coming from, while helping find a solution. The narcs just listen to find loopholes to place blame on anything other than themselves.

Be with people who want to fix the problems that arise along the way. Who choose to forgive you for the mistakes. Who choose not to hold it against you after there's been resolve. That is what a healthy relationship should be.

Healthy relationships are what we should expect. Rather than people who choose to manipulate, gaslight, and blame everyone else for the problems instead of taking responsibility for their own.

Who you are will show through any mask you have over time. The values you hold within yourself spill through when you speak. Sometimes on purpose, and sometimes unknowingly. It reveals so much about yourself, and who you truly are. So even if you try to hide yourself, the truth always come out.

Be careful not to allow the small mistakes to re-define the entire make up of a person. No one deserves to be looked at as if the person they are is the mistake.

Kayil York

Quit running back to the past.
It won't give you anything different
than the destruction that's already happened.
It won't change because you twist the
story of the truth in your head.
It won't give you anything better
than what's already been given.
Quit running back, those steps
are already marked in the concrete
and you can't take them back.

Good people still make mistakes.
It doesn't make them a bad person.
It just makes them human.

Kayil York

Trying is not a waste of time, it is how we learn how to succeed in the midst of failure.

Not everyone you lose will be an easy loss.
Sometimes it's a relief because of how toxic the relationship was. Sometimes it's a joy to let go of the very person who brought you down. And sometimes it's the hardest decision you can make. Just because you choose to let them go, doesn't mean you stop loving or caring about them. Sometimes it feels like it'll break you or kill you because you have such an attachment to them. You can love someone very much and the best thing you can do is let them go when you outgrow them, or they outgrow you. Hanging on to dead roots will not bring life back to it. It isn't easy losing people. But sometimes it is what's required for your next step in life.

Kayil York

She doesn't wear dresses
made from bitterness.
It isn't her color.
Nor does she play with
truths that are set before her.
She calls it how she sees it,
to get to the bottom of the issue,
so, forgiveness can take root despite
the desire to stay hurt.
She doesn't wear dresses
made of bitterness.
Don't assume you know
someone you only look at
through your level of perception.

Never seek revenge.
It is what small people do.
Rise above, wish the ones
who have hurt you well.
Then continue to live
your life. No one is worth
stealing your peace over.
All it will do is have
power over you and hold
you back from the life
you are meant to live.

Kayil York

Some people need you only to fill a hole
they need to fulfill themselves with healing.
And as time goes by, the truth of
their needs will come out, while you
become the collateral damage in
their war in finding themselves.

Maybe it was my fault. Maybe I was expecting too much because the years that had already gone by had allowed me to do just that. Maybe it was your fault too because you stopped giving anything at all. Claiming you couldn't, but darling, we both know that isn't true. In the end though I didn't matter who's fault it was, it was ending because it was time.

The hard part about not wasting your time with people is that you don't really know who someone is until you start spending time with them. Even then, there is a certain amount of time that must go by for someone's true colors to come out. That's what makes it so hard to see if someone is meant to stay in your life or not.
Because you don't know until you know.

When it comes to boundaries, you already have the means of making those decisions on how you want to create those boundaries. You just have to find the means within yourself to set them without letting the fear of their opinions cloud what you're doing to protect yourself.

I let you go because it needed to happen.

When I said I would leave you be, I meant it. We had reached a toxic level and there was no going back to how things used to be. It was evident everywhere I looked; you had backed off. Instead of telling the truth, you gave excuses without trying to solve the problem with me. It was you and I against the problem, not us against each other. I did my best to figure it out, while you were dead set determined to make me the problem.

I let you go because I was done fighting, done trying to share my feelings and the things I noticed that changed. I was done trying to resolve our problems so we could move on. I was done feeling like I was the only one who made everything go up in flames. I was done with it all. Because you can honestly only do so much to try and make things work with someone. And if they are not honest, not upfront, or real with their intentions and feelings, it is not a relationship worth pursuing or keeping.

If you listen to what your gut is telling you, what your instincts are showing you, you can save yourself a long road of heartache.

And that's what I did.

I used discernment, trusted my gut, and made the difficult choice to let you go. And amidst the healing and growing, I have had peace ever since.

I understood because I am always understanding. The damn grey zone is a battlefield. The black and white share other colors that make it impossible to just see things one way. You see every single side, every scenario that could have brought this ending. You see the tiny details of when things started to change, the messages that are few and far between, the lack of communication, the pull back, the inevitable alteration that is becoming reality.

You feel the distance taking place before anything is verbalized. You sense the shift, and at that point things may be too far gone. The important lesson in this shifting is that you need to let go of the hold you're trying to have over the crumbling, so you can allow what is going to happen, happen.

Kayil York

Some realizations hit too close to the core.
It's like a nick in your heart that stings or burns.
Either way, you know it hurts.
And you can't help but touch it because it hurts.
While you beg yourself to be ok.
To be ok with the cut.
Because it's there, it's happened already.
And all you can do now, is live with it.
But either way, it's frustrating to know
the wound is there, when we didn't
want it in the first place.

The truth is, not everyone deserves your presence, your time, your energy or a piece of your heart. Yet, that's what we do. Because maybe if we hope enough, it'll be the time you can say you're happy to witness humanity giving back the hope we've willingly been giving so long.

Kayil York

Sometimes it's not about being right.
It's about looking at the situation,
recognizing the way your words hurt
the other person and apologizing.
Sometimes it's just the way you
chose to speak is what hurt the most.
Not the point of being right.

Be willing to compromise sometimes.

Not every wrong action should result in walking away. Not every argument means the relationship is over. Not every harmful word was meant to be said to hurt you. Not everyone is out to destroy your heart on purpose.

Not everyone is trying to ruin your faith in humanity. No one is perfect, by any means. Mistakes will be made that will hurt and break your heart. But it doesn't mean you write them off completely. Sometimes you fight through the hard times. Because that's all it is.

A hard time.

Not every relationship should fail because your heart gets broken. It's just how life works. You choose someone, a friend or a lover. By choosing them, you choose to walk beside them. Seeing every part of them. Revealing your own self in the process. Discovering new ground on the same road. Showing your own flaws. Revealing your own shortcomings.

So, compromise. Work together. Because most of the time, the mistakes being made are not a reason to destroy what's taken so much time to build.

The hard part about therapy is all of the pain that gets brought up. The point of therapy is to recognize the roots that have split and bled. To find the pieces that aren't in the right place, and to move them back to where they belong. To find a greater understanding of who we are and who we have become despite or in spite of our traumas and greatest pains. The hardest part about talking about it, is that we have to talk about it.

We have to talk it out of our system, because holding it in causes the greatest harm and will hold you back from progressing the way you're meant to. Allow yourself to cry as it hurts, to embrace the feelings of despair and crushed dreams. Shattered hopes and unmet desires.

After that, you learn how to accept what has happened to you. You give yourself a chance to breathe finally, because the weight has done nothing but take your breath away.

And it was finally time to breathe. There is only so much time you should allow to go by before you face the hard things, accept that they have happened to you, heal the pain, so you can live your life to the fullest without the past weighing you down.

If they keep stringing you along,
there can be no trust.
When there is no trust,
there is no stability.
And without stability,
there can be no certainty.

There is a severing of the heart that happens
the more promises someone breaks to you.
It's losing the hope they gave you again,
after it's been taken away before.
Attempting to glue back what they broke
many times, before.
Trying to restore the faith they made you feel
bad about for not having.

The hurt is deeper, the trust is obliterated,
and the reason for you to stay and try
is no longer needed.

This is every reason you need to move on.

It was the turning point.

There are moments in your life that shift you, so you don't go back. It's the moments that break your heart while setting it free from bondage. It's the moments that hurt so much yet you're absolutely sure is the right thing to do. It's the moments that you decide who you are, and how you're setting your boundaries, because people have done nothing but walk all over them your entire life.

And this was my turning point.

When I said you wouldn't hear from me again,
I meant it.

The times that lead us to this moment was an unraveling, a tearing that I could not prevent, because the grace was never there on your side. And I made the decision that I can't be involved with anyone who can't give grace because their ego is larger than the desire to keep the relationship.

This was that important moment.
And I haven't looked back.

It's not that you care too much.
It's that you gave your all, bared your soul, and put everything you had into the person you love.
Only to be trampled on and left to feel like who you are was never good enough for them.
That… is brutality.

Sometimes you need to uproot everything that's not good for you and purge yourself of all the wrong things so you can make enough room for the development of good things.

Pain is still pain.
Hurt feelings are still hurt feelings.
Even if they think you're overreacting, doesn't mean the pain is any less painful. Not everyone will be able to understand your perspective or your sensitivity to certain things. Don't try to explain it to them because they don't care. Don't try to justify to them why it hurt you because they'll just finds reasons to make those reasons seem invalid.
If it hurts, it hurts. Period. Don't let anyone make you feel that your feelings are not important just because they don't understand them.

Taking space is necessary sometimes in order to get yourself in a better place. Being around the ones who caused the hurt in the first place can prevent you from healing. It's ok to take some distance to breathe. To recenter yourself so you get back in the right head space. Don't apologize for that. Everyone deserves time and space to heal from the things that broke your heart.

Kayil York

Anything you give room to in your heart,
you give power to.

It's ok to be upset if someone showed you who they truly were. Sometimes we like to see people through the lens of our perception instead of seeing them for who they really are. Be grateful when they show you who they are, so you're not illuding yourself into believing they are someone they in fact are not.

I think it's ok to check in with yourself and with someone you trust to tell you the truth. We can't be perfect. But it doesn't mean we aren't doing our best. Someone who claims things about you that aren't true are projecting themselves. Or are just lashing out in anger. If you do recognize something true about yourself in those words, then confront them head on. Work on yourself in those areas so you can be better. We aren't perfect and always have things we need to work on. Break the pattern, change the cycle, and choose to do what it takes to change what needs to be changed.

Imagine the future you envision for yourself.
Then look at what you're doing right now.
Is it serving you?
Is it helping you reach your goal?
Is it helping you succeed?
Are you furthering your reason?
Are you doing what is necessary to answer your calling?

If you aren't, then shift your course, change your situation.
Everything you do has an impact on your future.
Make sure it is helping fulfill it, rather than taking time away from it.

I have given so many people the power to destroy me, because I chose to trust without conviction, without a second thought and without doubt. My intentions were pure, and my reason was sane. But without fail, destruction was done. And every time was a lesson, but one that would not allow me to stop giving because of the wounds they left me with. There are times when you learn and act accordingly to change the outcome, and then there are times when you learn while still choosing to do the same thing over again because you know it's the right thing to do.

Be careful who you vent your frustrations to, your secrets, your thoughts, and your heart, because not everyone is there to listen and help. Some are there to learn your weaknesses so they can one day use them against you. That's why it's important to be wise and discerning when it comes to who you let into your circle.

You will not always be someone's first choice. They may love you and tell you how much they care about you. But there will always be someone that they will choose over you. Even though they may be your first choice.

It was a new kind of darkness you introduced me to. It was unlike anything anyone else had showed me. It was the opposite of who I was, and that's when I realized I could not live in a world where the things I touched ended up withering. I never wanted to be like you. That's what earned my silence in the end. And that was something you could never understand.

Unlearning is not impossible; it is merely the process of relearning what you thought to be normal. Some of the things you are taught as you grow up could be considered your normal but really are not. That is why it is important to read, learn, and grow as you age so you are able to recognize the areas you may need changing in. As well as the mindsets that need shifting.

I was a lighthouse that lit up your darkness that you couldn't bear to see. And instead of walking out of your shadows, you burned another bridge to keep your comfort with your demons.

Kayil York

Until you care for the things going on inside your heart; your pain, your internal struggles, those wars— you will not heal correctly.

Your heart was not made to be hidden in shadow. But it was not made to be played with either. So don't be afraid to share your heart, but don't allow anyone to mistreat you for their own personal gain. Because you deserve the greatest love, the utter happiness and glory of life that it brings.

Kayil York

I will let this pain go.
But I can't undo the
changes it's done
to my heart.

I am proud of the weaknesses that built up my strength. There were many times I should have been knocked to the ground to stay down. I should have stopped swinging my fists and gave into the defeat. But I kept pressing through until I got back on my feet.

The sad part was that they would rather destroy something they know had the potential to be good because they couldn't stomach the courage to own up to their own wrong doings.

—ego is a very powerful drug

*Stop damaging other people
because you have yet to heal—
you are causing unnecessary
pain.*

I stepped away from it all, from life, from everything. Because I reached the point where I was not taking care of my heart, and it had been too long since I gave my soul a chance to breathe from the chaos. I wasn't going away forever; I just needed some time to finally be me again.

Don't carry your pain for too long.
It becomes an unnecessary crutch that will
hold you back from the things that are
meant to make you feel light.

Kayil York

You sat under my skin
like you came to church
to repent.
You looked the part-
acted the part-
But when it was time to get real,
you turned into a devil that just
wanted to feast upon my heart.

-people are not as they seem

One of the worst kinds of knowing's is the solitude of our own feelings. The way we hold them beneath our chest and in the ways we allow them to drown our minds. Roaring over how we justify (fear) keeping the locks on our hearts.

I guess the trouble with it all is the certainty
that I was never unsure of my love for you.
But you made it difficult to see if you truly
loved me or if it was just a whim of feelings
until the next person comes along.

It is a great tearing.
letting go of the ones
who no longer want you.

Kayil York

Sometimes it hurts too much
to write everything down.
Yet, it's the only way
I know how to heal myself.

I'm going to cry again.
And there will be more days
to follow where it will be filled
with tears.
But it is only because I want
so much to heal what I have
let hurt me for far too long.
It is time to be whole again
again, and again.

Kayil York

I grow from the things
that destroy me.
It's a beautiful way
to begin again.

I have come a great distance to be who I am.
I have done things I am not proud of and made
decisions sometimes I wish I could change.
But I don't have regrets.
I am better because of the things that broke me.
I am better because I chose not to let the terrible
things make me a hard person.
We all have a choice as to how pain
and heartache will shape us.
And I hope you choose to allow it to make
you into someone you come to love.

Kayil York

And you should
let the pain have its day.
Let it shake you.
Allow it to hurt.
And then, you should notice
all the ways it has helped you
open your eyes to see destruction
in a whole new light.
Because it is a glorious thing
to know that after all the pieces
are put back together, there is new hope
in this new start.

I was giving up on you.
I wasn't giving you words in persuasion
anymore.
I wasn't begging for your attention.
I was giving up on you.
I wasn't waiting for you to notice,
Although half of me was.
I wasn't wasting wishes
on burnt out stars anymore
I was giving up on you.
I wasn't spending nights calling you
hoping you would answer.
I wasn't crying myself to sleep either,
I was giving up on you.
Even though you had already given up on me.

Strength.
Being able to stand in the same room
as your trigger while not letting it
get to you like it holds all the power.

They will accuse you of causing it all. Their pain, the source of disrespect and malice. The reason they change for no one. The reason they trust no one. They will give the lies the light so you can burn from their rage, scorch in their fire breathing hole of darkness. They will claim their allegiance to their demons like they somehow fill the holes, keeping them madly sane, while providing the appropriate barriers to keep themselves locked behind closed fences. Their hearts scream cold and black and emotionless. Because it's easier to keep things buried rather than confronting them. Because it's easier to accuse others of their mistakes than it is to actually admit to their own. Because the dark is a better place to stay, since it's where they've set up camp their whole life. Basing everything on the need to survive.

We met at a time of desperation. Both of us needing something from the other. The first year of it all was just what I expected it to be. Filled with phone calls, texts, skyping, hang outs and sleepovers. It became real so quickly. Sharing secrets and dreams, tears and demons. Days flooded to months like a blur, and it was a friendship I was proud of. Because it felt right, it felt good. And I trusted you fully. I didn't want anything from you but a connection. I was nothing but honest with you about that connection. You spoke freely about your feelings on certain situations, as did I. You gave time as did I.

But then it went wrong too fast. Something I didn't want to happen. I don't even know where we went wrong to be honest. It's just life happening when there are cancellations. Doesn't mean there is disrespect. Because again, as you said it yourself, life happens, and things happen that are out of our control. And I can't do it all. So, setting you aside for a time that I needed to have for myself, was me respecting my limits. Not disrespecting your feelings. The problem I had was that you could not see that. You expected that for you, and I did that, so many times. Because you not only needed it, but you also demanded it. And the one time I needed to demand it myself, it was unacceptable to you. I needed understanding, for you to give me the benefit of the doubt. I had to step back, I had to stop giving to you for the sake of saving myself. And trying to explain that to you was like speaking to a deaf person. You had absolutely no understanding.

I moved out of the way.
Because somehow considering
me to be a roadblock was easier
than acknowledging the flaws
in my humanity.

Do not use your choice
to stay broken as a reason
to blame others for mistakes
that are not their own.

Kayil York

This year had taken so much from me that I didn't know how to handle it. But it taught me the value of asking for help when it all becomes too much. Because sometimes you need more than yourself to help you get through a broken heart. Moving into the new year, there is no new me. There's only a new perspective, a newfound healing, and a new road waiting to be paved so that I will step over what I used to trip on.

People who tell you to trust no one, have no business even attempting to be in your life. Because they sit and wait for you to mess up, then say you're the reason they trust no one.

She stood her ground this time. Because for too long she went by what others said, what they taught, and what they told her to do. This time she took hold of who she was, trusted it, and went with it. Because there comes a time when you need to count on yourself, on who you've grown into so you can be who you are, unapologetically. Bravely. You owe it to yourself to be all that you are.

You deserve to be earned, my darling.

Love is given, yes, but it is also earned. Because there is a truth in the kind of love that's real. The kind that sets your soul on fire, but also keeps it kindling at the end of the night. The kind that isn't all about the physical gratification, but the true connection of heart and soul and deep conversations. That is a trust that is earned by the consistent and brave. So, if they want you, make sure they do what they can to earn you.

Your healing takes time when you're in serious pain. There will be times where you will fall back into the hurt and it will consume you. But don't be discouraged, it doesn't mean you haven't made progress in your healing. It takes a series of breakdowns, crying sessions, and hurt feelings and the acceptance of those feelings to get to wholeness.

You have to go with the ebb and flow of your own process. Because everyone is different, and healing doesn't have a timeline.

Be easy on yourself when you fall back into the pain. You're finding your own way- and it's ok to move at your own pace.

Sometimes in the face of great tragedy, you just have to be brave enough to accept that the pain is already changing you. The journey has taken a shift. Your life has changed, and you will never be the same. Life hands us those moments and most of the time we have no idea why it had to happen to us. Or even how we're going to handle it. Because it hurts, it punched a hole straight through your heart. Leaving you with an empty space that could never be replaced. But we learn how to live with it. We may heal, but some holes can't be filled with what once was. And that is ok to hold that space for the love that deserves to stay.

It's ok to fight for your peace.
Even if that means removing people from your life that try to prevent peace from staying with you.
It's ok if fighting for your peace creates distance with others. Because at the end of the day, only you can create the space you need for the peace you desire.

These days are the hard ones sometimes.
The ones that pull at you every which way,
asking more of you than you have to give.
These days are the rough ones.
The moments where the tears have built
themselves a home within your sanity-
just waiting for the wall to erupt into pieces
to spill over and smooth out the edges.
These are the hard days, but they are
not ones that last forever. You just have
to pull whatever bit of strength you
have within you to make it through.

It is not weakness when you choose to start over.
It is mature recognition that the way you were living was not serving you, challenging you, or making you better. And the moment you decide to step into that transition is the moment your fears become the collateral damage in this fight to being everything you were meant to be.
That victory is worth every sacrifice.

I never lost anything
I thought I should have had.
What is here, was meant to be.

If you looked at her again you would see the changes clearly. The hard parts of her soul have softened with time because she chose to have peace over bitterness.

Her broken heart she picked up, placed the pieces in God's hands and asked Him to repair her back to wholeness. And the way she made her past mistakes she worked daily on not being that way anymore.

Sometimes all it takes is the willingness to change because you want to be better.

So, if you choose to look again, you'd see her in a whole new light.

It's ok to want the simple things.
To cherish your every moment.
To live without being in front of the camera 24/7.
To be present without the need for being on your phone.
To not worry how many likes or comments you're getting.
To want real personal connection face to face
with the people you love.
I hope this year you can prioritize the important
things that truly matter, starting with the simple things.

Kayil York

After it crushes your soul, that is when the meaning will rise to the surface. The soul scent will make itself known to you, revealing the heart of who you are when you're pressed to pieces.
You are not done, my darling.
You are only just beginning.

People will only *try*
at their level of ***want*** to.

It was Brave because you had your heart broken before and you still chose to love once more.

It was Brave because you weren't sure how you could trust someone like that again, but you knew trying again was the only way to overcome your fear. It was Brave because you decided to be better over bitter. It was Brave because even in your darkest moments you gathered enough strength to keep going even though you knew it would have been easier to stop.

It's ok to leave people behind.
Not everyone is willing to step forward to heal themselves when the going gets rough. But that doesn't mean you have to stay behind with them. Nor should you make apologies for choosing to heal the parts of you that broke in the process.

Kayil York

The truth is that finding yourself after losing yourself isn't going to be easy. Because you don't just go back to who you used to be, that person stopped being you the moment you took that first step forward out of your old skin. You'll have days where you'll miss your old self and it may feel like you don't know how to be this new you, but you were called to die to yourself multiple times throughout your life, so you know what it's like to begin again with a new heart, a cleansed soul, and an open mind to the new possibilities waiting to be discovered.

I protected my heart by changing the parts of me that needed to fall away. For it is better to shed the old pieces that no longer serve you in order to grow into the next best version of you.

Kayil York

You're more beautiful for having been broken.
Because it made you stronger and braver in your
move to heal your soul.

I promise this won't last forever. You will work your way through this pain into healing. It will be too heavy to carry some days and other days it won't hurt so much to get out of bed to embrace the opportunity for a new day. You will have overcome what you thought you couldn't so you're able to change the course of brokenness to be one of hope and healing. Just keep going; continue, push through and fight for yourself. You're more than worth it.

Kayil York

To hell with the easy.
My bones were not shaped without the reckless
aching of what pain is meant for. The muscles of
my soul were not ripped apart without giving love
in honest. Nor was my heart built with the bricks
of resiliency without the world shattering me into
pieces from time to time.
If the best things in life came easy, you wouldn't
appreciate them the way you should.

I didn't want your heart to be a casualty in this war, but you didn't understand that I needed to be without you.
Sometimes you must do what's best for your heart even though you know it'll hurt to let go of what you wish could stay.

Kayil York

When you return,
the world will look different.
As it should, because the heart of you broke itself
open to become irrevocably changed.
To never return to the way it was before.

I love the difference
this change has made in me.

People can't touch who you are now.
Because the changes you've incorporated
into your life have made you evolve into someone
entirely new.
So even when they try to dig up who you used to
be,
it won't make a difference because you are not
bound to where you have been the moment you
knew you couldn't stay where and who were.

I found my peace with the situation after months of sleepless nights and endless questions keeping my heart sick with anxiety.

It took time because I had to break down the layers of you to understand that the ending was what I knew from the beginning. You were not different from the others; nor were you after the truth of having a real connection. Just a reminder that the sincere nature of cultivating something real isn't what most people want. They would rather watch it fall while adding you to their wall of unrealistic expectations while naming you another broken heart instigator.

I found peace with it all by not letting go but cutting off the weeds surrounding my heart attempting to squeeze the life from me. Through the years I have rummaged through the destruction of broken relationships and have learned that no one is worth sacrificing your peace for. Because the amount of time and understanding it takes to achieve internal peace should never be compromised for people who only want to make a puppet out of a heart with pure intention.

It won't be as hard to go through the difficult things. Not that it won't be uncomfortable and hurt while you go through it. But it won't come quite as a shock. You'll break again, but you'll be able to heal a little faster so you can move forward better than the way you used to. You'll bleed a little, but you'll know how to patch yourself up with a better understanding of how vital the balm of forgiveness is.

People won't surprise you anymore with the way they are because you already expect it. You'll walk with a little more peace because of the journey pain took you on to know what your worth is.

The process of growing comes with sacrifices, but the wisdom and knowledge you gain will help you face life in a different light with a new line of sight.

Growth-
Reaching a point in your strength where you don't struggle to contact the ones who left you. Because their absence showed you what it meant to step into the life they were holding you back from living.

It was never out of the hardness of my heart that I refused to have a relationship with you. It was the wisdom of past experiences that have made me understand the importance of setting boundaries and how important keeping your peace is.

And the more peace you took from me, the more confident I was that cutting ties with you was the best decision I could do for myself.

Being left out does not always mean you're not wanted. Sometimes you need to stand in your solitude to understand that your calling is not meant to have certain people involved. So instead of seeing it as you are being left out, look at it as God keeping the wrong people from interfering with your journey.

Thank you for rejecting me
thank you for bailing on me
thank you for not caring
thank you for not being there when I needed you
thank you for ghosting me
thank you for not making an effort
thank you for not treating me right.

I needed to understand that your rejection was meant to show me that my worth is greater, and that this redirection is meant to get me back on the track you took me off of.

Your character always speaks for itself.
If it's only one person accusing you of being someone you're not out of the many who truly know you, they are merely projecting who they are.
Do not take it to heart. Just keep being you and walk on. It is not worth being the collateral damage in someone else's war they continuously fight with themselves.

You will have to come to terms with the fact that not everyone is going to forgive you. The ending may not have gone the way you wanted, feelings were hurt, words were said that you can't take back, and the irreversible damage has been done.

If you find yourself in this place, try to accept the apologies you will never receive and choose to move forward; because healing is meant to find you in places they won't be able to be a part of.

There was never going to be a starting over, because you always wanted an ending. Because it fit your life better, to have everything around you controlled to the degree of manic. And if anyone ever questioned you, there was no need for them anymore. That meant you making him sacrifice his family for the sake of being comfortable. For the sake of your own selfish agenda. For the sake of keeping your demonic grip in the places you know we would tear it from. You think you may have won, but you didn't. And let's not forget who removed themselves from the equation, yes it was *you*, my dear. Let's not forget who couldn't get over *their* pride to mend things. Again, it was *you*. Let's not forget the wicked and horrid things you said in order to hurt as deeply as you could. And for that, your presence is not welcome anymore. Nor is the presence of the one you stole from us. Toxicity is your love language - destined from the beginning we were never meant to get along. So the cords were cut, the silence was given, and peace was finally able to settle back into our lives.

It truly is amazing the kind of peace you receive when you cut the demonic, the toxic, and the unbearable from your life.

And if you ever decide to attempt to re-enter into the lives of the ones I love, you can guarantee I will be there with my guard up ready to fight. Because no one will come forth easily after the last time your malice was heard. If you don't come back, all the better. Because we don't need anyone who is only around to hurt, destroy, and condescend. Anyone is better off without that.

It takes a long time to get through certain pains that have destroyed pieces of your life. Even then, years can go by and the heartache of what can never be anymore can sit heavy on your chest, digging deeper into the places it already sticks to. I have to go back to the times and remember what it was like to try with a monster that was only out to destroy. Hearing the clear disdain, the evident evil dripping from her lips, was a red flag flapping so vigorously it was hard not to miss the way she waved it. Proudly. Arrogantly. Those conversations were difficult to get through because after the first few words I knew it was not going to end well. No matter how many words were said, no matter how many times I call for reconciliation, it is met with a wall of abrupt termination.

The gut-wrenching thing when it comes to family is the way you were so tightly knit, woven into one another. No matter what, you will always be stitched into the fabric of one another. And the difficult part of life is when you're forced to tear that piece from yourself. *To rip*, despite the blood rushing out, *to remove*, despite the tears making way for the burial of the toxic dead weight. What follows is the complete anger because of the steps it took to get to this place where they give you no other choice but to rid them of their title of *family*.

Kayil York

Though blood is thick, it can fade to water through the lens of letting go.

Understand that the worst part about healing is how much pain must be exposed. You must open yourself up, tear at the seams if you must. Because you can only hold things in for so long before they start to invade in spaces they were never meant to live in. Your soul is a cavern; the things that happen to you in this life gather there as a collection of pieces. Some of those things are the happy parts that bring sunshine and smiles that warm you. But other times storms come in to destroy you, breaking off pieces here and there. Reorganizing and rearranging your heart in ways you're not used to. And the impact builds up pain that flows in and out of the shore of your caverns. The difficult side of making it through the repercussions of the storm, is rebuilding what was destroyed without allowing it to travel to places it doesn't belong. Healing is rough because of how much it changes you. It shows the annihilation of your old self, of who you once were. Confirming you can never go back to the way it was before. But that does not mean you can't become a better version of who you're meant to be. Your soul will hold your pain until you heal it, and without letting go of it you will continue to hurt. Then the hurt will turn into rage; rage into bitterness, and then into a coldness that hardens your heart. Life is filled with so much heartache, and it is important that we learn how to maneuver through the difficult, so we can live with purpose and with courage.

You are a steady reminder of how mistakes can burn cities to the ground without remorse. A reminder that not everyone gives chances like they should. Or the necessary grace needed for being human. You are a constant reminder of why it is important to know who you are. Because no matter what your opinion was, you will never know me based on the assumptions you curated in your head. You are a steady reminder of how arrogant someone can be when they choose to hold things against you instead of forgiving. A hypocrite who projects their own mistakes while denying their own ability to be wrong.

You are also a steady reminder of how getting rid of toxic people can improve your quality of life. Because I don't spend my time wondering when we go back to the way it was before. It was over. We had finished. Our final moments filled with words of distortion and difficult emotions. Of lies that you would never confess to. Of truth that the future could no longer hold what needed to fall away from one another.

You are a heavy reminder, a startling wakeup call that some people are just not worth the trouble of sacrificing your own wellbeing for because it was never something they even considered to care about.

You won't be bulletproof all the time. There are times when the shots will go straight through your heart; completely obliterating you into pieces. Shattering the armor you worked so hard to build in order protect yourself while drawing the deepest amount of pain from the wounds it left behind.

We don't always get it right because we give out trust to the ones we love. But sometimes it is the ones we love the most that know how to hurt us the deepest. It will be difficult to patch yourself up while healing the trauma that's been embedded into the fiber of your every thought. But you have risen from the ashes many times before, so don't be afraid to face the pain again so you can be brave and live without this holding you back from the healing you deserve.

I remember how much it hurt when I realized you were not coming back. I thought that kind of aching would not cease, I thought the blood coming from my heart would for sure makes its way through to soak my shirt. Revealing every part of me in the pieces I was truly in. But I also remember the way I was able to let go of you day by day as if piece by obliterated piece was slowly repairing the holes that were punched into my chest. The bruises you covered my soul in became not so noticeable. At some point I was able to wake up without the throbbing in my head. You may have taken a lot from me, but it never compared to the way I was able to put myself back together without you.

Remember the ones who left you when you needed them the most. Because there will come a day when you rise so far off the ground from where they left you. And they will try to come back into your life as if the pain they inflicted was never there. But you will remember the way they left and that will be the strength you need to keep your position above what is truly beneath you.

I used to be afraid of letting people go, because holding on has always been my strong suit. It becomes difficult each time to adjust to the hole that people leave when they are no longer a part of your life.

I stopped being afraid when I understood that when you let go of certain people, it is healing to your soul. Not everyone is good for you, not everyone is for you, and not everyone wants the best for you. So even though it may hurt to untangle yourself from ones that you love, it will bring back the life they slowly sucked from you. It is the best way to take care of yourself so you're able to heal and move forward in loving who you are and not being ashamed because it could not keep who did not belong.

Sometimes you don't have to try. Not because you don't think they're worth it. Not because you don't love them. Not because giving up was what you wanted to do. But it's because you know the connection isn't right, no matter what way you try to make it work. No matter what direction you try to twist it. No matter how many times you change your vision to attempt to see something else. It won't work. When it's not right, it's not right. And when it's not right, it won't work. And when it won't work, don't try to make it. Because trying to put together two pieces of what don't belong, will only cause pain and destruction on both sides. And love was never meant to be painful when it's true.

I wasn't perfect through it, but at least I tried by giving what I could. So, when it was time to throw the towel in, guilt didn't eat at me. Because I tried, I fought, and I burned for you. Even though you didn't do the same for me.

As I listen to the pieces of your heart, I feel the twinge of pain within my own. Hoping and praying that you see that your tears are watering the brokenness, washing the blood from the wounds, giving meaning to your suffering. These days will be difficult to maneuver through because it has never felt more unbearable. But the strength in your bones that you are growing into is enough to help you make it through.

I promise you.

Kayil York

And when I feel like burying myself,
I kick up the dirt and shove it into my soul so I can
start growing from the pieces they left my heart in.

Stay away from people who show you how toxic they are yet refused to admit it by projecting their toxicity on you.

You've got to do better at understanding her.
She dresses every day in strength to face the day,
but there are times where life literally tears off
every piece, she had protecting her, coming home
completely stripped down to her most vulnerable
self. And the exposure is like a wave of ocean
seeping into torn blisters. So, if she's not herself,
give her some grace. Because you have no idea
what it took to get her home after each day strips
her to the bone.

Remember,
you were never meant to
apologize *to* or *for* the ones
who made you bleed.

Kayil York

The healing comes light, as tender as a simple
touch. It comes in the form of a seed to plant itself
within you. You see, healing is not simple, it takes
the tourniquet off the places where pain made its
mark and forces you to see the way your heart was
torn. And it is never easy to look at how badly
your wounds are bleeding and feeling how much it
hurts. That's why healing is slow. Because the
levels you have to go through, the pieces you have
to put back together, and the strength to make it
through the unbearable, is a journey that weighs
heavy. So when healing comes, it does not force
itself into you, rather it is there when you a ready
to use it to help yourself. Even if it's one piece at
time.

Not everyone is going to understand your feelings or the place that they come from. No matter how the pain presented itself. Pain is still painful. If they don't understand, know that they don't need to. Your pain is justified because it is yours. No matter who is incapable of understanding it.

Kayil York

Over the years I would bend so far back to accommodate everyone else that I would nearly break. I was good at giving too much while sacrificing my own wellbeing because I thought that was what you're supposed to do. That was the norm. But now I have learned it is healthier to put up some boundaries. To say no when you haven't had time to fill your own soul back up. It's ok to step back and not be there for anyone but yourself. I've learned this with great toil and brutal perception. Now I've straightened my spine to be a little bit harder so I can walk a little taller. I've stopped giving away too much of myself so I'm not stuck in the situation of not knowing who I am because I couldn't set up the necessary boundaries needed to protect my heart.

The strength in our soul
rests in the scars
of our heart.

I'm begging you to come back to yourself. You are standing there on the precipice of where you are and where you will be if you step forward without the ground to guide you. You have risen off the ground getting through all the hell that you've gone through. You have never gone too far from yourself. You may come back completely renewed, completely transformed, and completely new. But it is never too late to come back from the journey that kept you isolated. When you've fallen and risen back up from the pain that kept you down, there is a new kind of clarity that brings you back to yourself. You are not what you've done. The mistakes you have made only contribute to how glorious your comeback will be. You may stumble getting back up off the floor, but you're still making a move to come into the healing that has been calling you home. It is never too late, no matter the time and no matter how far away you are. You can always come back home.

Forgive them anyway,
Expecting apologies that won't come because at the end of the day the state of your soul and the peace it holds is more important than the unforgiveness that wants to linger.

Kayil York

Thank you for all of your support and love. This book was written to help you through whatever difficulties you make be facing. I hope that it finds you where you are, holds you where you are, and heals you where you are. I also hope that it helps you know you can move into who are you becoming. You are a valuable human, your soul is irreplaceable and who you are is everything.

All the love,

xx – Kayil York

Printed in Great Britain
by Amazon